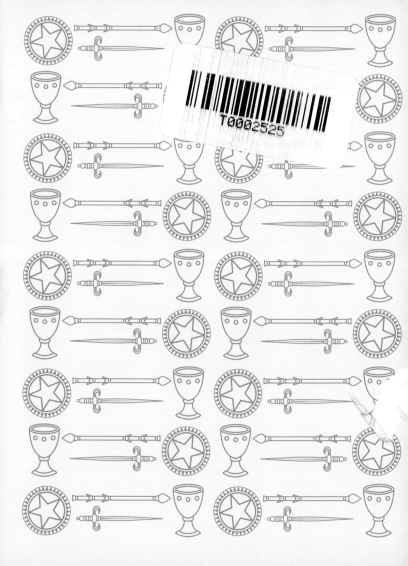

THE
LITTLE BOOK OF
TAROT

THE
LITTLE BOOK OF
TAROT

*Discover the Tarot and find out
what your cards really mean*

LIZ DEAN

CICO BOOKS

LONDON NEW YORK

Please note that Tarot cards are intended to be treated
responsibly and with respect. Generally, they are not suitable
for children. The way one reads Tarot cards may be guided by
the information in this book, but ultimately the interpretation
of the cards is up to the individual, for which neither the
publisher nor author can be held accountable.

Published in 2023 by CICO Books
An imprint of Ryland Peters & Small Ltd
20–21 Jockey's Fields   341 E 116th St
London WC1R 4BW   New York, NY 10029

www.rylandpeters.com

Abridged from *The Mystery of Tarot*, first published in 2003

10 9 8 7 6 5 4 3 2 1

A CIP catalog record for this book is available from
the Library of Congress and the British Library.

ISBN: 978-1-80065-186-9
Printed in China

Editor: Slav Todorov
Senior designer: Emily Breen
Illustrator: Melissa Launay
Senior commissioning editor: Carmel Edmonds
Art director: Sally Powell
Creative director: Leslie Harrington
Production manager: Gordana Simakovic

FSC
www.fsc.org

MIX
Paper from
responsible sources
FSC® C106563

CONTENTS

Introduction 6

1 HOW TO LAY THE CARDS

2 INTERPRETING THE CARDS

INTRODUCTION

THE TAROT IS A STORY, as all good mysteries are. Its reputation has the romance of the Romanies, the power of the Italian dukes who commissioned the first cards, and a 600-year-long popularity. One episode saw the cards being carried by persecuted missionaries as a secret code; another twist had the Tarot denounced by the Church as "the Devil's picture book." Yet universally the Tarot has been a tool for those seeking enlightenment.

Learning Tarot is like learning a language, but it uses symbols as a way to explain itself. The occultist A. E. Waite, in his *Pictorial Key to the Tarot*, says: "Given the inward meaning of its emblems, [the cards] do become a kind of alphabet which is capable of indefinite combinations and makes true sense in all." It is hoped that this book inspires you to learn how to use the Tarot and benefit from the insight that this ancient mirror of life provides.

The suit of Cups relates to events of an emotional nature.

Tarot iconography frequently features symbols of life, death, and rebirth.

HOW TO USE THIS BOOK

The first chapter shows you how to lay out the cards for a reading, ranging from the simplest three-card spread to more detailed layouts, such as the Celtic Cross and the Tree of Life. There are examples of genuine readings to demonstrate how the cards work in action, and how they relate to—and illuminate—each other during interpretation.

Chapter two offers interpretations for all seventy-eight cards: the twenty-two cards of the major arcana and the fifty-six of the minor arcana. For the major arcana there is a passage on the card's symbolism, and another that decodes the astrological symbols that appear on many Tarot decks. Each interpretation presents card combinations.

1 HOW TO LAY THE CARDS
TAROT READINGS

IT IS IMPORTANT TO CHOOSE A DECK that you really like. You will have it for a long time and you have to live with it; people rarely give away their cards, so unless you inherit an unwanted Tarot deck, you will need to purchase your own. There are so-called traditions that dictate that you should not buy your own cards, but that they should be bought for you as a gift. Do not worry about this—choosing cards is such a personal experience that it would be difficult to rely on someone else to do this for you.

If you have not bought a Tarot deck before, try one that has illustrated "pip" or numbered cards, such as the Rider Waite Smith deck. The images on the card will stir your memory if you already have some familiarity with the Tarot, or will help you learn the card meanings from scratch. However, decks with geometric suit designs for the numbered cards are preferred by some readers who feel limited rather than inspired by minor arcana pictorial imagery.

Always treat your Tarot cards with respect. Keep them wrapped in a dark cloth, preferably in a box or drawer. They are personal to you, so do not leave them on display for others to touch. It is important that they absorb your energy as you continually handle them. This is why some Tarotists recommend sleeping with a new deck under your pillow for the first few weeks after purchase.

WHEN TO READ THE CARDS

When reading for yourself, make it a habit to read when you feel that you don't need to. This may sound contrary to the traditional view of needing a reading because you have decisions to make, or other pressing events about which you seek clarity. However, reading the cards when you don't have an urgent question can help you develop a more detached attitude.

Start by reading for yourself once a week. Vary the spreads that you use—start with a three-card spread and progress to more complex arrangements as you gain confidence. And pay attention to the patterns of cards, because you will find that over time certain ones recur.

READING REVERSED CARDS

While shuffling, some cards naturally reverse. A reversed card is upside down, and in a tarot reading its meaning is different to that of a card in the upright position. Often, reversed cards can have more negative meanings, but several, such as the Five of Cups, have a more positive interpretation. You can choose to use reversals or not. Many readers do not read reversals—if they arise in a spread, they simply turn them the right way up before beginning to read.

PREPARING FOR A READING

Shuffle the cards as you think of a question or an event that you would like illuminated. Then take the shuffled deck and, with your left hand (traditionally this represents the hand of fate), cut the deck into three piles. Choose one pile, then place the other piles underneath it as shown below (in this example, pile 3 has been chosen). Your chosen pile should be on top. If you are reading for someone else, ask them to shuffle the cards so that they imprint them with their personal energy. Then ask them to choose a pile. Take this pile from them, then gather up the remaining two piles, as explained above. When the deck is ready, lay out your cards in a spread (see overleaf). Turn the cards face up from left to right or right to left.

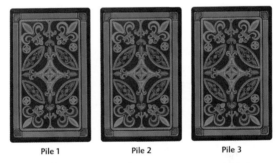

Pile 1   Pile 2   Pile 3

2 Bottom   1 Middle   3 Top

THREE-CARD READINGS

Threes make a story: a beginning, middle, and end. You can start by using just three cards to create a Tarot story that describes the past, present, and future.

Card 1: Past
Card 2: Present
Card 3: Future

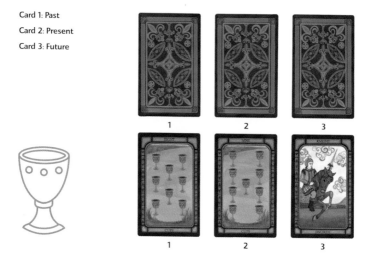

The querent wanted to find out about future relationships as she had just left a long-term partner. The cards drawn are the Eight of Cups, the Nine of Cups, and the Knight of Swords.

The Eight of Cups is in the past position, which shows that there has been dissatisfaction in an established relationship.

The Nine of Cups shows that this is a good time to meet a new partner.

Her future is the Knight of Swords in shining armor: a professional, charming individual. Events will speed up, and there is drama. To find out more about the Knight, we chose an additional card, the Ace of Wands. This indicates beginnings.

SAMPLE READING: MONEY, WORK, AND LOVE

Card 1: Money

Card 2: Career

Card 3: Love

1

2

3

The querent did not have a pressing question, so we used three cards for insight into her three key life areas: money, work, and love. The cards drawn are the Magician, the World, and the Emperor.

Because three major arcana cards have been drawn, important change can be expected. The Magician appears as the money card. This is a creative time for her—her horizons are expanding. She is near the end of a particular phase of work; she may even be thinking of changing her career.

The Emperor is the querent's love card. In a woman's reading, the Emperor traditionally denotes her husband. Here, it represents her long-term partner, who could give her stability as she undergoes major changes in her career and finances.

THE HEART AND HEAD SPREAD

This reveals the spiritual, intellectual, and emotional aspects of your life, along with a card that acts as a key to the whole reading.

Remove all the minor arcana cards from the deck, then shuffle and cut the remaining twenty-two cards, laying down four as shown. Read card 4 first, and interpret the other cards in the light of this.

1

3

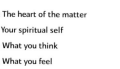

Card 4: The heart of the matter

Card 1: Your spiritual self

Card 2: What you think

Card 3: What you feel

2

4

SAMPLE READING: LEAVING WORK

The querent is taking early retirement from work. The cards drawn are the Chariot, Justice, the Hermit, and Temperance.

CARD 4: The heart of the matter is Temperance. She is working hard, weighing up her finances until her layoff payment, and dealing with potentially precarious individuals whom she needs to rely on right now.

CARD 1: The Chariot represents the querent's spirituality and her hopes for herself. This card reveals that she will make sure progress.

CARD 2: Justice appears in the thinking position, which is apt given that the querent wants her decision to be justified, and wants to be fairly treated financially and have her past work acknowledged.

CARD 3: The Hermit reveals how the querent feels. It shows that she feels a little alone on her path to seek the life that she wants.

1

3

2

4

SAMPLE READING: MAKING A COMMITMENT

The querent has a good relationship with his partner, with whom he does not live. He would like some insight into issues of commitment for the future. The cards drawn are the Empress, the Sun, the Moon, and the Devil.

CARD 4: The heart of the matter is the Empress. This is the querent's partner. She represents home life and the desire for love, stability, and, perhaps, a family.

CARD 1: The Sun in this spiritual-self position reflects the querent's hopes for joy and security.

CARDS 2 AND 3: The Devil and Moon signify thoughts and feelings. The Moon casts doubt on the querent's sunny hopes, while the Devil reveals a fear of commitment. These two cards link with one another, because they reveal subconscious doubt and an awareness of a pending decision.

THE STAR SPREAD

Card 1: The present

Card 2: Feelings

Card 3: Thoughts

Card 4: The heart
of the matter

Card 5: The subconscious:
what is hidden and
will surface

Card 6: What you desire

Card 7: The outcome

The Star is a popular spread with Tarot readers, and it can be particularly insightful when you use only the major arcana cards. Shuffle, cut, and lay out the cards as shown above. Interpret card 4, the heart of the matter, before the other cards.

SAMPLE READING: WILL THE PAST BE PUT TO REST?

The querent has been looking back at past issues that have been troubling her for some time. She wants to know if she can resolve and heal the past.

CARD 4: The querent's card is the Tower. It shows that her beliefs or way of living are being undermined. However, this sudden collapse will be liberating in the long term, after the shock subsides.

CARD 1: This shows where the querent is at present, and here the Death card makes an appearance. Along with the Tower, card 4, Death is confirmation that major changes are underway.

CARD 2: The card in this position represents the querent's feelings about her situation, here symbolized by the World. She knows deep down that she is ready to move on, and that by rights she needs a fresh start.

CARD 3: The Hermit reflects how the querent has intellectualized her situation. The card also suggests she needs to follow her own path.

CARDS 5 AND 6: Card 5, the Devil, is the querent's subconscious at work. She will need to make a mature decision if she is to make progress; she may be tempted to stay where she is, perhaps repeating old patterns of behavior. This decision is important if she is to achieve the ambition of card 6, the Star, which reveals her known desires. She would love to feel inspired and hopeful, and revitalized rather than drained.

CARD 7: The Magician is a great card here, because it shows that the outcome will be positive. The Magician is a wonderful symbol of energy, creativity, and in some cases travel; he deals with the present and looks to the future. Unlike the Hermit, the Magician shows off his talent to others, so it appears as if the querent finds a way to express herself, rather than be overly reflective.

7

6

5

4

3

2

1

THE PAST, PRESENT, AND FUTURE SPREAD

Card 1: Your present circumstances

Card 2: The past

Card 3: Past challenges

Card 4: Lessons and guidance

Card 5: New influences about to enter your life

Card 6: How they will affect you

Card 7: The outcome

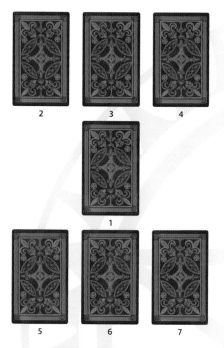

This seven-card spread is a good preliminary to the Celtic Cross (see page 24). The pattern of the spread consists of two three-card sequences for the past and future, with a single card for the present. Shuffle and cut the cards, dealing seven cards face down from the top of the deck as shown.

The querent did not have a specific question, but wanted a general overview of past, present, and future influences surrounding her career.

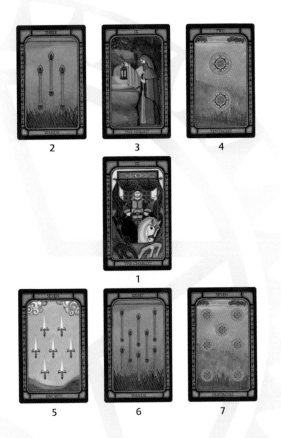

CARD 1: The querent's present circumstances are represented by the Chariot: through determined effort, she is forging ahead in her career. We moved this card to one side and laid four more cards around it (see Variation, opposite).

CARD 2: The past is represented by the Three of Wands. This shows that the querent's past work has been recognized by others.

CARDS 3 AND 4: The Hermit reveals past challenges, and here suggests working alone. The Two of Pentacles shows she learned to find better balance and more interaction.

CARD 5: The Seven of Swords reveals new influences that are about to enter the querent's life. The Seven shows conflict and the need to use her intellect to negotiate some challenging situations.

CARD 6: The Eight of Wands illuminates the impact that these new events and feelings will have. It shows that the hard work of the Seven of Swords pays off, and she will be rewarded with opportunities to shine and possibly travel.

CARD 7: The Seven of Pentacles is the outcome. The querent will need to stay focused and work hard for promotion. The message here is to persevere.

VARIATION

Four additional cards were chosen to surround card 1, the Chariot: The Sun, Star, Knight of Cups, and the Knight of Wands. It is likely that the querent will see some rapid changes very soon, since the two Knights indicate the speeding up of events. The Sun and the Star signify reward and inspiration. The Knight of Cups can also mean a lack of action. If this is a new boss, he may not give her adequate support with the difficulties that await with the Seven of Swords, card 5 in the main reading.

THE FOUR ASPECTS OF THE PRESENT

1: Present circumstances

1a: Highest potential

1b: Work and projects

1c: Money

1d: Movement

1a

1a

1d

1

1b

1c

THE CELTIC CROSS

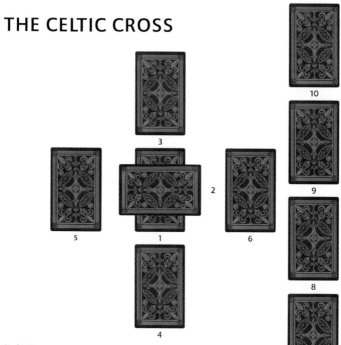

Card 1: Your current circumstances

Card 2: What is helping or hindering you

Card 3: The best you can expect at present

Card 4: The foundation: hidden factors

Card 5: The past

Card 6: The near future

Card 7: How you see yourself; what you can do

Card 8: Outside influences

Card 9: Hopes and fears

Card 10: The outcome

The Celtic Cross is a traditional and popular spread that explores general life influences and events. This layout can vary: some readers place Card 3 to the right of the cross and continue clockwise. Shuffle and cut the deck as usual, then deal ten cards from the top as shown.

SAMPLE READING: CAREER OVERVIEW

The querent is a painter who is nearing the end of a difficult commission. He wants to know if his work will be well received, and if more commissions will result.

CARDS 1 AND 2: The Devil is crossed by the Five of Wands. The Devil shows that the querent feels tied to an unsatisfactory situation that is causing worry and conflict. The Five of Wands reveals that he is under pressure, and faces a situation that he has not previously encountered. Together, these cards show that he has felt restricted and unrewarded in his work. The challenges of this commission are new to him. There may also be a problem with a contract here, suggested by the Devil.

CARDS 4 AND 5: The Lovers and the Seven of Swords looks at past circumstances and any hidden elements that may be contributing to the present situation. The Lovers shows that the querent has made a commitment to himself and his work, and may have taken a risk to do so. The Swords card can indicate a lack of trust prior to the work beginning, which has now magnified in the form of the central card, the Devil.

CARD 3: Justice is the best that the querent can hope for at this time—he will be fairly treated in a testing situation, and any contractual issues should be finalized to his satisfaction.

CARD 6: The querent's next move is represented by the Knight of Wands. This reveals that events will speed up, and new offers of work should arrive. The Wands are cards of creativity.

CARD 7: The Star reveals how the querent will see himself at this time. He can recover his creativity and inspiration.

CARD 8: The card in position 8 shows attitudes around the querent, and the general influences impacting upon him. He will feel at one with the world, and feel happier and more secure financially, symbolized by the Sun.

CARD 9: The Four of Wands reveals the querent's hopes and fears. This card shows that he can hope for appreciation and establishment.

CARD 10: The outcome to the querent's present situation is represented by the Four of Swords. This shows a time for healing and recuperation after struggle.

We can also look at the combined meaning of the two Fours here, cards 9 and 10. Two fours together traditionally indicate that there will be a good time of stability ahead.

8

3

10

5

2

6

9

1

4

8

7

THE TREE OF LIFE SPREAD

Card 1: Kether: spirituality

Card 2: Chokmah: what is
to be realized

Card 3: Binah: what you
understand

Card 4: Chesed: What
supports you

Card 5: Geburah: tests

Card 6: Tipereth: The issue
or problem

Card 7: Netzach: desire

Card 8: Hod: Conscious
thoughts

Card 9: Yesod: The
unconscious

Card 10: Malkuth: outcome;
what materializes

This meditative spread is helpful when you have a lot going on in your life. Each card represents a sephirot, or energy center, on the Tree, which has various interpretations, just some of which are given here. Shuffle and split the deck as previously described (see page 11), then lay out ten cards in the sequence shown.

SAMPLE READING: CAREER OVERVIEW

The querent is hoping to sell her city apartment to move to her home in the countryside. She wanted some clarity on whether the move would work out for her.

CARD 1: SPIRITUALITY
The Seven of Cups shows that the querent sees many possibilities, but she needs a clearer vision of how living away from the city might materialize.

CARD 2: WHAT IS TO BE REALIZED
This card position also shows the querent's relationship with the men in her life. The Six of Cups reveals reunions with old friends and those people from her past.

CARD 3: WHAT YOU UNDERSTAND
The Three of Cups shows that she appreciates her relationships with women in her life, and she will soon be meeting supportive friends.

CARD 4: WHAT SUPPORTS YOU

Temperance shows that the querent needs to look after the detail just now—she must tend the balance of her life.

CARD 5: TESTS

The Seven of Wands shows that the querent hopes that all her hard work will pay off.

CARD 6: THE ISSUE OR PROBLEM

The position of card 6 also reveals what is in the querent's heart. Here, she has the Ace of Swords reversed, showing a time of frustration and delay before she can relax and enjoy her country home.

CARD 7: DESIRE

The Eight of Swords shows restriction on the romantic front, which is not surprising given that all the querent's energy is being dedicated to work and home at this time.

CARD 8: CONSCIOUS THOUGHTS

The Three of Pentacles can show tradespeople. The meaning of this card here may be the building of a little empire.

CARD 9: THE UNCONSCIOUS

The Tower is the querent's card of the unconscious or hidden issues. On a practical level, she is leaving a safe fortress for the unknown and feels vulnerable.

CARD 10: OUTCOME; WHAT MATERIALIZES

The Page of Cups brings invitations, conversations, and ideas. The querent will soon receive good news.

THE HORSESHOE SPREAD

This is a classic spread to call on when you need an answer to a specific question. The Horseshoe can have either five or seven cards; a seven-card reading is shown here. Shuffle and cut the cards as usual, then lay them out as shown.

Card 1: The past

Card 2: The present

Card 3: Future conditions

Card 4: The best path to follow

Card 5: Attitudes around you

Card 6: Obstacles

Card 7: The outcome

1

2

3

4

5

6

7

SAMPLE READING: WILL MY FINANCES IMPROVE?

The querent has had to take out loans to finance his debts. He is self-employed and needs to pay tax in the coming months, and is doubtful if he can keep up his repayments. The cards chosen are the Ace of Pentacles, the Seven of Wands, the Ace of Swords, the Three of Pentacles, the Empress, the Ten of Wands, and the Moon.

CARD 1: The Ace of Pentacles shows that the querent has been successful with money in the past. He may have had a windfall or other cash gift.

CARD 2: The present shows the Seven of Wands: he is fighting off demands on his time and money, and will need to work hard to get the security that he hopes for.

CARD 3: The Ace of Swords reveals that he will succeed, provided he has a strategy.

CARD 4: The Three of Pentacles shows attention to detail, hard work, and creativity. If he presents ideas to clients, he will be rewarded with new work.

1

2

CARD 5: The Empress reveals that others will be generous and understanding. The downside of this card is that people may assume that the querent is not struggling, since they are used to him being financially capable.

CARD 6: The Ten of Wands predicts that the querent may be overburdened with responsibility. This may also reflect his attitude: things may get on top of him and he may feel paralyzed by indecision, rather than driven to act to resolve his debts.

3

4

7

CARD 7: The outcome is the Moon, which reveals a crisis of faith and indecision, as indicated by the previous card. The querent therefore needs to act now to improve his situation, rather than wait until the repayments become a serious burden. The Ace of Swords shows that he can extricate himself from his debt and win.

6

5

THE YEAR AHEAD SPREAD

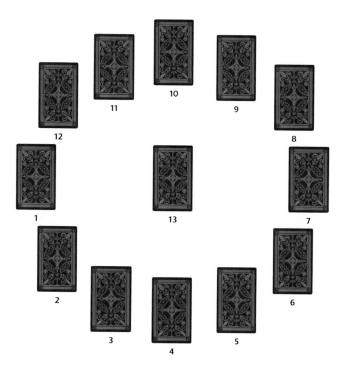

Cards 1–12: Card 1 represents the first month from the date of the reading

Card 2: This shows the events of the next month, and so on for twelve months

Card 13: This reveals the tone of the year ahead

SAMPLE READING: WHAT THE NEXT YEAR HOLDS

In the Year Ahead Spread, one card is laid out for each month of the year, plus a central card 13.

CARD 13: The theme of the year ahead is revealed by the Five of Wands. This shows the need for the querent to stand firm and stay true to her principles.

CARD 1: Month one has the Seven of Pentacles, which represents ongoing work and the potential for success.

CARD 2: In month two, the Page of Wands brings some welcome fun and fresh inspiration.

CARDS 3, 4, 5, and 6: The next four months reveal a run of major arcana cards initiated by Death, which shows an ending and a new beginning. The querent will undergo some major changes during this time. Justice shows that she is rewarded morally. The Hermit heralds a time to recuperate. The Strength card shows that she will need to be patient, and even emotionally strong in order to support others.

CARD 7: The Star brings creative opportunities and vitality. Her dream will come true.

CARD 8: Month eight brings the Two of Cups and an intimate partnership, born from the happy environment of the previous card, the Star.

CARD 9: Month nine is a time to look forward to, as friendship, celebrations, and lightheartedness prevail with the Three of Cups.

11

CARD 10: Month ten reveals the Four of Pentacles, showing proud achievement, satisfaction, and deserved rewards for work.

12

CARD 11: Month eleven brings the Ace of Pentacles; this will be a great time for career and money.

CARD 12: Month twelve shows a reversal of the good fortune of the Ace, but this can mean personal disappointment or feeling socially distanced rather than a financial lack.

1

2

3

10

9

8

13

7

6

4

5

THE MONTH AHEAD SPREAD

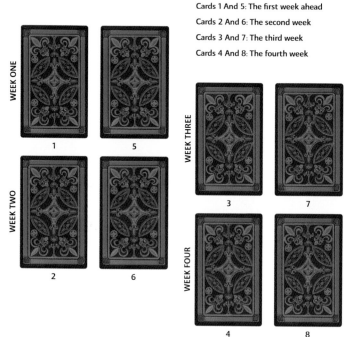

Cards 1 And 5: The first week ahead

Cards 2 And 6: The second week

Cards 3 And 7: The third week

Cards 4 And 8: The fourth week

WEEK ONE

WEEK TWO

WEEK THREE

WEEK FOUR

1

5

2

6

3

7

4

8

SAMPLE READING: WORK FOR THE NEXT FOUR WEEKS

The querent wanted to know how her work would progress over
the next month.

WEEK ONE: The cards drawn are the Six of Cups and the Ace of Pentacles.
This will be a profitable and possibly innovative week workwise.

WEEK TWO: The Nine of Cups and the Star show that it is likely that
she will be recognized for her ideas.

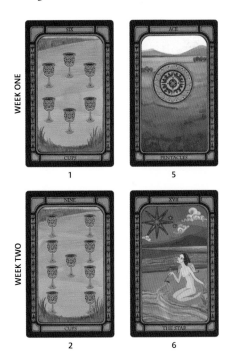

WEEK THREE: The Eight of Swords and Temperance reveal that now the querent needs to put her ideas into action and manage challenges along the way.

WEEK FOUR: The Four of Cups shows that the querent will feel that her life is back in kilter, but there may also be a trace of irritation or boredom—maybe because issues from week three do not get resolved. This may escalate into a battle, shown by the Three of Swords, which clears the way forward.

THE WEEK AHEAD SPREAD

This spread is an ideal way to gain insight into an important week ahead. Shuffle and cut the cards as usual, then lay them out following the arrangement shown, beginning with a Significator card, which reveals the theme of the whole week.

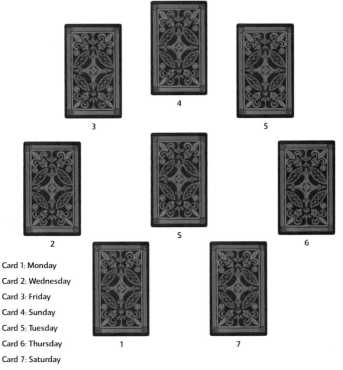

Card 1: Monday

Card 2: Wednesday

Card 3: Friday

Card 4: Sunday

Card 5: Tuesday

Card 6: Thursday

Card 7: Saturday

S: Significator card

SAMPLE READING: WHAT THE NEXT WEEK HAS IN STORE

The querent wanted to see how she would prosper financially, creatively, and socially during the week ahead.

THE SIGNIFICATOR (S): The significator card is the Ten of Wands. This foretells an incredibly busy week; the querent may take on too much and feel overburdened with responsibility (some readers prefer to shuffle and cut the cards again when this card arrives: see page 128). However, the overall outlook—given the spread of cards—is very positive.

MONDAY (1): The Eight of Wands brings great news and happiness. This is an auspicious day for work and expressing her talents.

TUESDAY (5): The Knight of Pentacles reveals that Tuesday is fortuitous for getting things done. It may not be inspiring, but progress is assured.

WEDNESDAY (2): Judgment symbolizes the summing up of a series of events before moving on. It is likely that the querent is coming to the end of a project, and will assess what has been achieved.

THURSDAY (6): The Ten of Cups shows great reward and joy, which is usually connected with a community or group of people.

FRIDAY (3): The Chariot. After the summing up of Wednesday and Thursday's happy endings, Friday sees the querent take up the reins once more to move forward.

SATURDAY (7): The Three of Cups crowns the sixth day, bringing harmony and love.

SUNDAY: (4) The Nine of Cups is the card drawn for Sunday. This Nine is traditionally the "wish" card of the minor arcana, so this is a day on which the querent's dreams can come true.

3

4

5

2

S

6

1

7

WHAT TO DO IF YOU CANNOT MAKE SENSE OF A READING

1. You can ask the querent to shuffle and cut the deck again. If the first cards are right, some or all will reappear in the second reading.
2. Don't look up the card meanings. Go with your intuitive response to the images.
3. You may feel hesitant if the cards are "bad": the Tower, the Devil, or Death, for example. Although they might seem traumatic, these cards often signal release and new beginnings.

2 INTERPRETING THE CARDS

THE MAJOR ARCANA

THE TAROT JOURNEY BEGINS with card 0, the Fool, and ends with card XXI, the World—beginning again with the reborn Fool. It is a continuous cycle of birth and regeneration. The innocent Fool experiences the other twenty-one cards as landmarks and tests as he seeks completion.

THE FOOL'S STORY

DISCOVERY: THE FOOL TO THE CHARIOT

The Fool is zero, an innocent who sets the wheel of the Tarot cycle in motion. He encounters I, the Magician, the alchemist who shows him the magical potential at his fingertips. With the Fool's growing awareness of his environment, he then turns his attention to his earthly and spiritual parents. These are II, the High Priestess—the goddess aspect of his mother—and III, the Empress, who takes care of his earthly needs. Similarly, his father the Emperor, IV, makes the rules; the Emperor's spiritual counterpart, the Hierophant, V, gives him an education. Card VI, the Lovers, is the first test of the Fool's autonomy, for he must choose between the parental bond and a relationship with a partner. When he meets the Chariot, VII, he realizes his freedom and risks dealing with the world alone.

THE MAGICIAN

THE LESSONS: JUSTICE TO TEMPERANCE

The Fool now encounters Justice, VIII (in some decks, numbered XI). He is judged by others and must account for his actions. The Hermit, IX, teaches him how to be alone and seek out what he needs, away from his peers. The Wheel of Fortune, X, takes him out of his ego with the realization that he is at the mercy of the greater power, Fate. In Strength, XI, the Fool learns gentleness when dealing with external opponents and internal conflict, and he must be prepared to make a sacrifice, which is symbolized by card XII, the Hanged Man. Death, XIII, brings both endings and renewal; the transition of spirit. Temperance, XIV, heralds the spiritual alchemist, and so the Fool learns to control his temperament and quantify the elements of his life.

FROM DARKNESS TO LIGHT:
THE DEVIL TO THE WORLD

The Fool's darkness is a power struggle between his lower instincts and his higher nature. He meets card XV, the Devil, and so greets temptation: having to choose between greed and generosity, lust and love. His success depends on his maturity. Yet whatever he envisages as being within his control, life has other plans. The Tower of his ego, XVI, collapses to make way for his connection to heavenly inspiration, in the form of the Star, XVII. Here, he realizes his goals and spiritual guidance, which take him to the creative sanctuary of the Sun, XIX. Yet his journey

is not yet complete. As the Fool has moved from the twilight of the Star to the full heat of the Sun, so he has had to endure the disillusion of the light of the Moon, XVIII, which exposes his deepest fears. He must again make a difficult decision that will ensure his progress. Judgment, XX, is the Fool's final calling to judge himself. He knows that his journey is almost complete. He has the World, XXI, to discover, all over again.

0 THE FOOL THE JESTER

The Fool is innocence. Poised to leap between one world and another, he risks the spiritual unknown. He appears in tarots as a beggar, a madman, a naive youth, and a jester. As the court jester can often articulate subtle or difficult truths, so the Tarot Fool may make his entrance into a reading to remind you of the intemperance and absurdity of life. And, as the jester plays off the crowd, so it has been suggested that he is set to experience the collective journey of all the cards in the major arcana cycle.

ASTROLOGY
The Fool's planet is Uranus, symbolizing independence and freedom.

UPRIGHT MEANING: BEGINNINGS
A fresh start; freedom from the constraints of the past; release from a pattern of events and taking risks—provided you can enjoy the freefall.

REVERSED MEANING: IRRESPONSIBILITY
In the reversed position, the negative traits of the Fool come to the fore. Naivety turns to immaturity and irresponsibility, warning that a spontaneous decision needs a rethink.

CARD COMBINATIONS
If the Fool is one of the last cards in a spread, she shows the completion of a phase or journey. With the Star, we see an inspired risk or creative or spiritual quest. With the Moon, impulsiveness leads to a crisis of confidence.

I THE MAGICIAN THE MAGUS

The Magician represents alchemy. In early Tarot decks, he may be seen as a merchant or artisan, whereas later decks show him as the alchemist, holding up his baton or magic wand. The Magician weaves magic with the four elements. On his table are the four suit symbols of the minor arcana: pentacle, cup, sword, and wand; earth, water, air, and fire are at his disposal.

ASTROLOGY

The Magician's planet is Mercury, ruler of communication. Mercury was the Roman god of magic, also associated with transformation, the essence of magic.

UPRIGHT MEANING: HUMAN MAGIC

The Magician's charmed influence indicates travel and creative projects, communication and energy. This is also an auspicious card for business dealings.

REVERSED MEANING: TRICKERY

The Magician reversed warns of cheating and false appearances, dreams without foundation, and even self-delusion.

CARD COMBINATIONS

Because he has the four suit emblems before him, the suit or suits that surround him can reveal the way in which his influence will be expressed. With the Ace of Pentacles, the Magician shows new financial opportunities, prosperity and establishment. With the Queen of Cups, the suggested meaning is happiness and new relationships. A relationship moves forward.

II THE HIGH PRIESTESS THE PAPESS

The High Priestess is the archetype of mystic femininity, the keeper of wisdom that is not easily expressed. In a reading, her appearance guides you to listen to your inner voice in order to move forward. She is the natural counterpart of card V, the Hierophant.

ASTROLOGY

The Moon is the planet of the High Priestess, signifying the inner world of secrets, emotion, and hidden knowledge. The crescent moon represents expansion, the waning moon decline.

UPRIGHT MEANING: INTUITION

Higher guidance. Take note of your dreams; nurture your desire for learning and seek out inspiration. In this aspect, the High Priestess is the teaching of your intuition.

REVERSED MEANING: SECRETS REVEALED

In this position, the High Priestess shows that a secret is about to be revealed. An additional meaning is feeling disconnected from your inner knowing.

CARD COMBINATIONS

With the Moon, a confidence crisis concerning a woman is revealed, or the need for intuitive guidance to make a key decision. With the Hanged Man, a spiritual perspective changes your viewpoint and calls for time away from a situation.

THE HIGH PRIESTESS

III THE EMPRESS

The Empress is Mother Earth. Serene and full-figured, she represents fulfilled potential: close and happy relationships, nurturing, and abundance. She is a goddess of love in human form, and all benefit from her magnanimity. She expresses herself through dialogue and her relationships with others.

ASTROLOGY

The Empress is associated with Venus, planet of love and fertility. Venus is concerned with what you value—relationships, material comfort, sensuousness, and sensitivity.

UPRIGHT MEANING: ABUNDANCE

Giving and receiving love comes naturally; money comes, bringing material comforts. You are supported and cherished, and can give to others unconditionally. The Empress can also predict a new relationship or a pregnancy, fertile ideas, and the positive influence of a mother-figure. This is a card of reassurance; know that you will grow and not falter in whatever you choose to do.

REVERSED MEANING: INSECURITY

Mothering becomes smothering when the Empress turns. Domestic bliss turns to chaos, so this card can reveal unhappiness at home. The thrust of the reversed Empress is scarcity rather than abundance.

CARD COMBINATIONS

With the Ace of Cups, a relationship or pregnancy that brings happiness is revealed. With Temperance, the needs of a family may be a source of tension.

III

THE EMPRESS

IV THE EMPEROR

The Emperor represents order and authority. His qualities are traditionally masculine: martialism (in some decks he wears a suit of silver armor), rationalism, and virility. He can be depicted in a desert; the lack of water, which symbolizes the emotions, establishes that reason, not feeling, rules him. His natural consort, the Empress, represents love, whereas the Emperor reveals power.

ASTROLOGY

The Emperor's sign is Aries, the Ram. Aries is ruled by Mars, a reminder of the Emperor's martial qualities as a defender of his kingdom.

UPRIGHT MEANING: FATHERHOOD, PROTECTION

The help of a father-figure, paternal love, and protection. This man will act, not pontificate, so his influence in a reading can reveal a life partner, guardian or parent, or someone in your life with wisdom and ambition. He is also a natural rule-maker; as a parent, he sets the boundaries, so his appearance in a reading can show a requirement to conform.

REVERSED MEANING: OPPRESSION

The reversed Emperor is deliberating and stubborn. He can therefore predict problems with parental or other authority figures. Overall, the card can indicate disorder and a need for structure and organization.

CARD COMBINATIONS

With the Magician, there is focused creativity as ideas take a workable form. With the Fool, a man with status brings adventure. With Strength, the Emperor brings further security.

IV

THE EMPEROR

V THE HIEROPHANT
THE HIGH PRIEST, THE POPE

The Hierophant is the upholder of spiritual tradition. His natural counterpart is card II, the High Priestess; the High Priestess works in secret, whereas the Hierophant works in public, mediating between Earth and heaven. He signifies faith and the quest for oneness.

ASTROLOGY

The sign associated with the Hierophant or Pope is Taurus, whose symbol is the Bull. A papal law or edict may also be referred to as a papal bull.

UPRIGHT MEANING: GROWTH

In the upright position, the Hierophant foretells teaching, spiritual advancement, and unity. This card shows you the sanctuary of a community, particularly in relation to education, such as a study group. For individuals, the Hierophant can take the form of a teacher-angel who watches over you from above.

REVERSED MEANING: RESTRICTION

When the Hierophant is in the reversed position, misinformation or a drive for unreasonable or unattainable perfection is revealed. Restrictive attitudes and the lack of a free flow of ideas casts suspicion and creates an atmosphere of mistrust. This can manifest as an organizational crisis at work or, for individuals, criticism that blocks projects.

CARD COMBINATIONS

It can be helpful to think of the Hierophant broadly as a symbol of tradition, unity, and self-development. Compare his qualities with those of the other cards that surround him. With the Ten of Wands, the Hierophant shows a feeling of being oppressed by authority/conformity. With the Lovers, this represents partnerships and commitment; love and marriage.

THE HIEROPHANT

VI THE LOVERS

The Lovers depicts a meeting of two hearts. The lovers are on the threshold of commitment, in a garden paradise. A decision is coming. The right decision can secure long-term happiness and gain, and this choice can relate to any situation as well as a love relationship.

ASTROLOGY

The sign of the Lovers is Gemini, the Twins. As the twins gaze at each other in union, so too they can turn away from commitment.

UPRIGHT MEANING:
A DECISION

An opportunity to move on, but in order to do so an essential decision needs to be made. When this card appears in a reading you go for what you want and consequently energy and vision are your rewards. In this sense, the Lovers is about commitment to love itself and for yourself, not just love for an individual.

REVERSED MEANING:
AVOIDANCE

When the Lovers invert, you go for the easy option, the path of least resistance, which gets you out of a troublesome situation. This, however, is temporary and takes you no further

forward in your relationships or goals. Another meaning of this card is temptation and possible betrayal.

CARD COMBINATIONS

When surrounded by positive cards, the Lovers reveals that you make the right decision regarding a relationship. When negative cards are close by, you take the path of least resistance that leaves important issues unresolved. With the Devil, this represents a decision that leads to entrapment or lack of fulfilment. With the Chariot, a positive choice brings progress, energy, and/or travel.

VI

THE LOVERS

VII THE CHARIOT

The charioteer represents energy and progress. With the previous card, the Lovers, a decision was made; the Chariot can therefore be interpreted as the resulting action of this choice. Life drives forward, and the charioteer must show steady purpose to gain the valuable experience that this journey offers and find his or her destination.

ASTROLOGY

The Chariot is associated with emotional Cancer, the Crab. Like the Crab with his hard shell and soft center, he must balance his head and heart in order to move forward.

UPRIGHT MEANING: PROGRESS

When the Chariot appears in your reading, action is the key word. Events are about to speed up and success is within reach. The card reveals movement in terms of a journey, yet often denotes another kind of departure from the familiar to the unknown—new work, moving on from a long-term relationship, or making significant progress in a creative or business project.

REVERSED MEANING: FRUSTRATION

The Chariot reversed is an arrogant charioteer, expecting unqualified support from those around him. Ego is in the way; this may be a reflection of your attitude, or you suffer due to others' egomania. On a literal level, the upturned Chariot reveals delayed travel and unexpected obstacles barring your path.

CARD COMBINATIONS

With Justice, a journey is morally justified; an outcome in your favor brings freedom. With Judgment, an era is near its end, and a new phase in life beckons.

VII

THE CHARIOT

VIII JUSTICE THE SCALES

After the Chariot comes Justice, who judges the charioteer's past actions. Justice represents decisions, righting previous wrongs, and restoring balance. Along with legal rulings, Justice also encompasses any situation in which we are assessed or judged by others.

ASTROLOGY

Justice is associated with Libra, the Scales. The Scales represent evaluation, fairness, and balance.

UPRIGHT MEANING: RESOLUTION

A legal matter is resolved. This is justice in its truest sense, because it takes no heed of your position. Therefore, the appearance of Justice may be a card of satisfaction or discomfort, depending on your circumstances; the truth is that a final decision is made that must be accepted. Taken positively, Justice in the upright position legitimizes an endeavor and predicts success in business and legal dealings. An additional meaning is divine law—guidance and direction from a spiritual source.

REVERSED MEANING: INJUSTICE

When reversed, Justice becomes a miscarriage of justice. You will know that you are right, yet the system goes against you. What you believe to be the truth is manipulated by others who are less qualified to fight your case. Fend off others' lack of faith and protect your integrity; choose new representatives or partners in business.

CARD COMBINATIONS

With Judgment, the practical and spiritual end of a situation. With the Wheel of Fortune, a resolution brings freedom.

IX THE HERMIT TIME

The Hermit is the seeker of knowledge. Often depicted wearing the habit of a monk, he chooses a lone path away from familiar comfort in order to pursue a personal quest. He is solitary rather than lonely, as his moving away from society is his choice. He brings a quieter pace of life.

ASTROLOGY

The Hermit's sign is Virgo, the Virgin. In this sense the Hermit is linked with card II, the virginal High Priestess, who also seeks and holds knowledge that is hidden.

UPRIGHT MEANING:
THE JOURNEY

The Hermit can reveal a need for reflection, healing, and discovery. You have to rely upon yourself, but you have the resourcefulness and integrity to find your way. This is an important card for self-knowledge and inner strength. It can reveal a physical or metaphorical journey that will bring emotional reward and spiritual learning. The appearance of the Hermit in a reading also relates to needing more time—to go at a pace that allows you to think clearly. An additional meaning is meditation.

REVERSED MEANING:
ISOLATION

The Hermit reversed reveals isolation that is imposed rather than chosen. You may be cut off from your usual support systems or feel cast out by a community; in this context, the lone hermit is sad and world-weary. Stubbornness or rash reactions, rather than thought, may see this hermit lose his way in the wilderness.

CARD COMBINATIONS

With the Hermit, time slows down, whereas the Aces and Knights of the more physically active suits (Wands and Swords) generally show that events will speed up. For example, the Hermit combined with the Knight of Wands would reveal a time of rest followed by intense activity. With the Ace of Pentacles, we see a new beginning after a time of healing.

THE HERMIT

X THE WHEEL OF FORTUNE FATE

The Wheel of Fortune marks the halfway stage in the cycle of the major arcana. After the soul-searching Hermit, the Wheel brings a new lesson—we get to understand what we can, and cannot, control; we can only go with its flow.

ASTROLOGY

The Wheel of Fortune card is associated with Jupiter, the planet linked with luck and learning.

UPRIGHT MEANING: A TURN FOR THE BETTER

The Wheel heralds improvement in your circumstances. Be open to change and new knowledge, and accept the gifts that life brings. Good fortune awaits. Spiritually, this card can also reveal that there's a whole side of life you haven't seen before, along with a calling to psychic or spiritual development work.

REVERSED MEANING: CLOSURE

Unlike many major arcana cards, the reversed Wheel is not negative. The natural order and disorder of the Universe may be beyond your control, but the focus is on how you experience the changes of fortune that it brings about.

CARD COMBINATIONS

The Wheel of Fortune indicates change, usually for the better. The cards that follow the Wheel reveal in which areas of your life this turn of events will be most keenly felt. With the Moon, a twist of fate brings about a crisis of confidence; a delay in adapting to altered circumstances. With Judgment, the Wheel shows events that accidentally work in your favor; synchronicity that quickly concludes important business.

THE WHEEL of FORTUNE

XI STRENGTH FORTITUDE

Along with Justice and Temperance, Strength (or Fortitude) is the second of the cardinal virtues to appear in the major arcana sequence. Strength is a lesson in dealing with dangerous forces and exerting self-control.

ASTROLOGY

Strength is associated with Leo, the Lion. In alchemy, the lion is a symbol of primary matter that can be transformed into gold, a metaphor for an enlightened state of mind.

UPRIGHT MEANING: TENSION

When upright, this card signifies the need for patience to deal with passionate forces that may be overwhelming. These may be from within—the lion can reveal that you are fighting your own shadow. Taming the lion, however, is not about takeover—more about self-control and courage when dealing with a challenging situation or impulse. In a reading, Strength also shows how to deal with a person whose outlook is very different from your own.

REVERSED MEANING: AVOIDABLE DANGER

Strength reversed can be interpreted as a weakness of will and an inability to take a genuine risk; rather than deal with discomfiting tension as you work out how to resolve a conflict, you try to deny the enemy all together. The message here is not to panic, nor retreat.

CARD COMBINATIONS

The Strength card is advice in itself, but when combined with other cards, it enables you to discover more about the nature of a test: this may be a test of will, a moral question, or inner conflict with your conscience or with your head and heart. With the Hanged Man, Strength shows an ongoing test of will that leads to a sacrifice or change of perspective. With the Fool, this can represent an attempt to resolve an issue, opting for escape rather than resolution.

XI

STRENGTH

XII THE HANGED MAN THE TRAITOR

The Hanged Man is a seeker of spiritual knowledge. Hanging upside down from a scaffold or tree, he is reminiscent of Odin, the Norse god who discovered the secrets of the runes by suspending himself from the World Tree for nine days and nights.

ASTROLOGY

The Hanged Man is associated with the planet Neptune. Neptune is the planet of fantasy, dreams, spirituality, imagination, and creativity.

UPRIGHT MEANING:
A CHANGE OF PERSPECTIVE

Waiting time; a period of suspension. Use this chosen or enforced delay to look at the situation another way. You may need to make a compromise to move forward and step away from immediate problems, if your new-found view on the situation requires it. Tarotist Alfred Douglas writes that the Hanged Man reveals a reversal of values, so an unorthodox solution to a problem may present itself. At a spiritual level, the Hanged Man shows spiritual development, guidance, and meditation.

REVERSED MEANING:
WASTING TIME

You may think that you are tied to one course of action, or feel you have become martyred to others' demands. Guidance from your unconscious and an openness to look at alternatives will liberate you. Release yourself from a contract with others or with yourself that cannot be fulfilled.

CARD COMBINATIONS

With the Hermit, time out for study or self-examination is revealed. With Death, a final resolution after a period of delay.

XIII DEATH

Death is the card of endings and transition. After him comes the Angel of Temperance, followed by the Devil, or the light of spirit and the darkness of earth. Death is interpreted in Tarot as deep change rather than physical death. When Death's influence is done, we can embrace new beginnings expressed in cards like 0, the Fool and I, the Magician.

ASTROLOGY

Death is associated with Scorpio, the Scorpion. Scorpio is linked with sex and death, the ultimate in beginnings and endings—the dual message of the Death card.

UPRIGHT MEANING: ENDINGS

The natural ending of one cycle of destiny; a moving away from old familiar patterns toward new opportunities. The card represents major life changes, such as relocation to a new home or job, the final end of a relationship, or the discarding of old beliefs and values. Remember that this transition is necessary to enable you to move on.

REVERSED MEANING: UNEXPECTED CHANGE

Death reversed may occur in a reading to show you that it is time to let go. You may have been holding on to outdated information or a relationship that you are continuing for the sake of it, although it is not fulfilling. If you cannot make the decision right now, this card indicates that change may be made for you. In this sense, Death reversed reveals unexpected events occurring: take this card as an opportunity to prepare yourself.

CARD COMBINATIONS

At its simplest level, Death shows change, so the surrounding cards help illuminate the nature of that change. With the Hierophant, for example, Death shows a spiritual beginning; the comfort of religion; Karmic lessons. With the Lovers, this can represent leaving an established relationship or lifestyle for a new passion.

XIII

DEATH

XIV TEMPERANCE

Temperance is the third cardinal virtue in the major arcana sequence, along with Justice and Strength (see pages 68 and 74). A maiden or an angel pours water from one cup or urn to another. She is a spiritual alchemist, integrating and harmonizing the varied essences of life. Temperance indicates resources, management, and tests—the need to balance conflicting demands on our time.

ASTROLOGY

Temperance is associated with Sagittarius, the Archer or Centaur. The glyph for Sagittarius is the arrow. On the Temperance card, water from the higher urn must be poured at a precise angle to fill the lower; in the same way must the archer have true aim.

UPRIGHT MEANING: RECONCILIATION

You may need to approach a challenging situation with scientific precision. It takes concentration to get the formula right when life feels like a continual balancing act with all its demands on your time. Success, however, requires commitment and effort. The card also suggests reconciliation, the resolving of financial issues, and spiritual guidance.

REVERSED MEANING: IMBALANCE

Temperance reversed indicates a tidal wave of trouble. This manifests as imbalance—past events may threaten to overwhelm you as your usual focus on the present dissolves. This card can also signify poor financial management or a general lack of resources. In love, difficult memories may surface, which may restrict a current relationship.

CARD COMBINATIONS

With the Four of Swords, recuperation after a stressful time. With the World, hard work brings deserved reward.

XIV

TEMPERANCE

XV THE DEVIL

Tarot cards often depict the Devil as Satan enslaving a male and female demon. One origin of the Devil is Pan, Greek god of excess (rather than evil). As the Angel of Temperance represents the potential of the higher self, the Devil represents the base, or lower, self. When the Devil appears, a decision must be made between our base instincts—fear, lust, greed—and our higher natures.

ASTROLOGY

The Devil's astrological sign is Capricorn, the Goat. Capricorn is ruled by Saturn, planet of time and restriction.

UPRIGHT MEANING: TEMPTATION

The Devil indicates temptation and obligation. The card reveals painful lessons: addiction, affairs, a moral debt, or other restriction, such as employment with little reward. At any point, however, you can choose to walk away; it is, after all, a situation that you may have created.

REVERSED MEANING: ENSLAVEMENT

The chaotic Devil may manifest as others attempting to manipulate your better side; ask for a little angelic intervention, and resist.

CARD COMBINATIONS

The cards placed around the Devil help reveal the nature of hidden energies around us. These can provide more information about the kind of temptation that the querent may be dealing with, and its impact. With the Ace of Pentacles, Death represents the temptation of money; a high price for security. With the Ten of Wands, this can highlight a moral dilemma or obligation that brings a burden of guilt.

XV

THE DEVIL

XVI THE TOWER THE HOUSE OF GOD

The Tower means unavoidable disaster: literally, an act of God as implied by the card's alternative title, the House of God or LaMaison Dieu. Like the arrow of love from Cupid or the scythe of Death, lightning can strike at any time. However, with ultimate destruction a new path is cleared for regeneration.

ASTROLOGY

The Tower is associated with Mars, the fiery planet of war. Mars expresses the violent destruction and aftermath of release that the Tower may bring.

UPRIGHT MEANING: DISASTER

The Tower represents sudden collapse. A bolt from the blue destroys what you have constructed: a lifestyle, business venture, relationship, or dream. Although The Tower signifies a fall, it does not suggest blame—only bad fortune that is unavoidable. In the aftermath, you can pick up the pieces and reclaim your ground. What you create now will have stronger foundations. Additional meanings include shock, and a breakthrough that illuminates the way ahead.

REVERSED MEANING: BLAME

The Tower reversed reveals disaster that may have been avoided. You may have created a basis for instability in your life, and now what you feared most has happened. Yet the upright Tower represents the sudden impact of fate, so you continue to suffer. Accept what has happened and forgive.

CARD COMBINATIONS

With the Star, a creative breakthrough; healing. With the Three of Swords, a relationship truth.

XVI

THE TOWER

XVII THE STAR

The appearance of the Star is a call from the cosmos, offering divine inspiration, hope, creativity, and healing. The card may be literal, depicting a lone female figure gazing up at a guiding star; or, as in many contemporary decks, a maiden holding two cups, kneeling to pour her water into a pool and onto the earth.

ASTROLOGY

The Star card is associated with Aquarius, the Water-carrier of the zodiac, associated with inspiration, ideas, and progress.

UPRIGHT MEANING: INSPIRATION

The Star reveals healing and harmony that are both physical and spiritual. Inner desires, which take form through your dreams, can now be consciously expressed. This card is therefore fortuitous for artists and for entrepreneurs. An additional meaning is spiritual or intuitive guidance.

REVERSED MEANING: CREATIVE BLOCK

The Star reversed can reveal a creative block, as with the reversed Magician (see page 54). You may not be able to fulfill your dreams just now; as starlight is bewitching, so is an impossible fantasy. While it is compelling to dream, be aware that you need to identify your real-life expectations.

CARD COMBINATIONS

A helpful reminder of the meaning of the Star in a reading is its star quality—it can show a major dream or need. The surrounding cards may reveal whether this dream complements or clashes with other major or minor events. With the Five of Coins, this shows a lack of resources; fear that a dream will fail. With the Devil, the Star represents a conflict between freedom and restraint; a test.

XVIII THE MOON

The Moon reveals a crisis of faith. As moonlight makes the world look different—surreal, even—this card depicts the landscapes of the inner world or subconscious mind. Old or unresolved fears surface; the dark or hidden aspects of our personality, like night wolves, come out to play. In the shadows, we experience the dark night of the soul before we meet the Sun, the next card in the major arcana cycle.

ASTROLOGY

The Moon's astrological sign is Pisces, the Fish. The association of the Fish with the soul and the element of water in which he dwells—representing the emotions—indicates the intensity of feeling linked with the Moon card.

UPRIGHT MEANING: DISILLUSION

The Moon shows disillusionment on the surface, but beneath lies a greater emotional turmoil. You may need to make a decision, but cannot trust what you see. Rely on your instinct; this is a time to follow your own wisdom. Additional meanings include mysticism, intuition, and messages in dreams.

REVERSED MEANING: AVOIDANCE

In the reversed position, the Moon reveals the danger of doing nothing. While this brings temporary respite, it cannot bring you resolution. In order to avoid a decision, you may be tempted to seek refuge in the past.

CARD COMBINATIONS

Helpful keywords when interpreting the Moon are illusion, disillusion, and confusion. This is an emotional card, so any card that follows the Moon in a reading can indicate how the querent deals with their emotions and moves forward. With the World, the Moon represents hesitation before the ending of a phase; a need to let go of the past. With the Sun, success after soul-searching; a release from uncertainty.

XVIII

THE MOON

XIX THE SUN

Like the two preceding cosmic cards, the Moon and the Star, the Sun holds powerful energy: here, this is joy, success, and rejuvenation. The depiction of a sun and child or children on early and contemporary tarots instantly communicates a radiant optimism. The Sun's life-giving warmth initiates renewal and growth; after the dark night of the Moon (see page 88) and the guidance of the Star (see page 86).

ASTROLOGY

The Sun's astrological association is with the Sun, ruler of Leo, the sign concerned with confidence and the ego.

UPRIGHT MEANING: SUCCESS

The Sun is always a welcome card in a reading: its heat permeates all aspects of your life, bringing love, children, energy, happiness, and success. This is a card of rewards, bringing whatever you value; so you may enjoy a vacation, receive money, or find your creative muse.

REVERSED MEANING: DELAY

The Sun reversed shows that heat and light, the gifts of the upright Sun, are just out of reach. You can envisage a carefree existence without worries about health, children, and work; this may take the form of a holiday

in the sun. It is important to keep the faith rather than give up, as this card indicates delay, not defeat.

CARD COMBINATIONS

Two keywords for the Sun are success and happiness. The cards that appear close to the Sun in a reading can show how a positive, productive phase is manifesting—in terms of relationships, finances, creativity, or simply recuperation. With the Ace of Wands, the Sun represents a venture that attracts practical support; ideas and conversations inspire creativity and new projects. With the Empress, a happy phase for a family in which success is shared; a new baby, a time of togetherness.

XIX

THE SUN

XX JUDGMENT

THE ANGEL, THE TRUMPET, FAME

As the penultimate card in the major arcana cycle, Judgment reveals the need for self-assessment before reaching card XXI, the World—which is concerned with completion and rebirth—and a return to card 0, the Fool. Judgment is a part of the renewal process, where we come to terms with the past before moving on. How do we judge ourselves?

ASTROLOGY

Judgment is associated with the planet Pluto. Pluto is concerned with identity and a quest for truth. Pluto was the Roman god of the underworld (the Hades of Greek myth). He expresses the need to examine the darker side of our natures, the message of Judgment, before moving forward.

UPRIGHT MEANING: RENEWAL

An opportunity for renewal; a time of beginnings and endings during which you gain perspective on the past in order to move on. Judgment can bring self-acceptance and reward, rather than regret; you may look back, but with pleasure. This card can also indicate second chances, to take a fresh look at an old relationship, or to revisit an existing opportunity.

REVERSED MEANING: GUILT

With Judgment in the reversed position, the chance to conclude a matter is delayed because you cannot confront a fear of change. This card can indicate guilt, and therefore soul-searching holds you back. It may be time to make peace with the past.

CARD COMBINATIONS

With the High Priestess, a situation is assessed intuitively rather than spoken aloud. With the Devil, it may be hard to move on and feel free in the world; you may need to make peace with yourself.

XX

JUDGMENT

XXI THE WORLD THE UNIVERSE

The World, or Universe—the final card in the twenty-two-card sequence of the major arcana—represents successful completion. Along with the Sun, it is one of the most positive cards in a reading. It brings the respect and acknowledgment of those who have witnessed your efforts.

UPRIGHT MEANING: REWARD

The upright World card reveals success and a special reward. One part of your life is reaching a natural conclusion, and you are primed with energy and optimism about the future. It is time to take an essential step into the wider world. This can be expressed through the opportunity to explore literally by traveling, or by embarking on a new direction in your profession or creative ventures. Completion and reward also bring opportunities for togetherness and celebrations.

REVERSED MEANING: DILUTION

The card in this position shows outdated values, or a situation that is unresolved or incomplete. You may miss out on immediate offers because you are unable to direct your energies to the present moment. This may be due to painful past issues, but there comes a time to pull away from familiar patterns.

CARD COMBINATIONS

When interpreting the World, consider that the card contains both beginnings and endings: in a reading, it can show that a new phase is already starting, so the cards around it may reveal how the querent will proceed and what their journey will bring. With the Fool, the World represents the start of an inspiring and successful phase that brings excitement and travel. With Justice, a decision in your favor brings satisfaction and closure.

XXI

THE WORLD

THE MINOR ARCANA

THE MINOR ARCANA COMPRISES fifty-six numbered cards that fall into four suits: Cups, Pentacles (Disks, Coins), Wands (Staves, Batons), and Swords. Each suit has ten numbered, or "pip" cards, from the Ace through to Ten, and four people, or Court, cards: Page, Knight, Queen, and King. Historically, the minor arcana pips bore repeat suit symbols to denote their number: two Swords, three Cups, or ten Pentacles, for example.

INTERPRETING THE MINOR ARCANA

The numbered, or pip, cards of the minor arcana are grouped together in this chapter, followed by sets of Pages, Knights, Queens, and Kings. The introductions to each set of cards offers guidance on the card's number or type and element.

INTERPRETING THE COURT CARDS

If you are a beginner, you may find the Court cards challenging, because they can refer to individuals. As you read you may get an intuitive flash, identifying a court card as an individual you know; but in general, it can be more helpful to look at the Courts in terms of personality types that also translate as an active influence. For example, if you were reading the Queen of Cups, this might traditionally indicate a sensitive, loving woman. If this is not manifesting in your

life as a person, then the card means that these qualities are important to you. The Court cards can also be read regardless of gender: a King, for example, can apply to a man or woman.

	UPRIGHT	**REVERSED**
CUPS:	Sensitive, kind, intuitive, imaginative	Uncommitted, overly idealistic
WANDS:	Passionate, motivated, communicative	Ego-driven, controlling
SWORDS:	Wise, direct, detached, instinctive	Ruthless, aggressive
PENTACLES:	Pragmatic, sensual, stable, generous	Untrustworthy, materialistic

INTERPRETING CARD PATTERNS

Some specific meanings have been attributed to the frequency of cards of the same number and type in a reading. A. E. Waite, creator of the Rider Waite Smith deck (see page 8), includes a list of meanings in his book *The Pictorial Key to the Tarot*. The list overleaf has been adapted from his original.

UPRIGHT

FOUR KINGS: acknowledgment, acclaim

THREE KINGS: consultation, advice

TWO KINGS: minor counsel

FOUR QUEENS: great debate

THREE QUEENS: deception

TWO QUEENS: sincere friendship

FOUR KNIGHTS: serious matters

THREE KNIGHTS: lively discussion

TWO KNIGHTS: intimacy

FOUR PAGES: potential illness

THREE PAGES: dispute

TWO PAGES: disquiet

FOUR TENS: criticism

THREE TENS: a new situation

TWO TENS: change

FOUR NINES: a good friend

THREE NINES: success

TWO NINES: acceptance

FOUR EIGHTS: a reversal

THREE EIGHTS: marriage

TWO EIGHTS: new knowledge

FOUR SEVENS: intrigue

THREE SEVENS: infirmity; vulnerability

TWO SEVENS: news

FOUR SIXES: abundance; advantages

THREE SIXES: success

TWO SIXES: irritability

FOUR FIVES: regularity; balance

THREE FIVES: determination

TWO FIVES: delay; awaiting a result

FOUR FOURS: a journey

THREE FOURS: reflection

TWO FOURS: insomnia

FOUR THREES: progress

THREE THREES: unity

TWO THREES: calm

FOUR TWOS: contention; conflict

THREE TWOS: security

TWO TWOS: accord, balance

FOUR ACES: favorable opportunities

THREE ACES: a small triumph; good news

TWO ACES: trickery

REVERSED

FOUR KINGS: swift movement

THREE KINGS: commerce

TWO KINGS: projects

FOUR QUEENS: bad company

THREE QUEENS: overindulgence

TWO QUEENS: work

FOUR KNIGHTS: alliance

THREE KNIGHTS: an encounter

TWO KNIGHTS: susceptibility

FOUR PAGES: hardship

THREE PAGES: idleness

TWO PAGES: society

FOUR TENS: event, happening

THREE TENS: disappointment

TWO TENS: justified expectation

FOUR NINES: exploitation

THREE NINES: carelessness

TWO NINES: a small profit

FOUR EIGHTS: error

THREE EIGHTS: a spectacle

TWO EIGHTS: misfortune

FOUR SEVENS: quarrelers

THREE SEVENS: joy

TWO SEVENS: faithlessness

FOUR SIXES: care

THREE SIXES: satisfaction

TWO SIXES: failure

FOUR FIVES: order

THREE FIVES: hesitation

TWO FIVES: reverse

FOUR FOURS: walks abroad; attention

THREE FOURS: disquiet

TWO FOURS: dispute

FOUR THREES: great success

THREE THREES: serenity

TWO THREES: safety

FOUR TWOS: reconciliation

THREE TWOS: apprehension

TWO TWOS: mistrust

FOUR ACES: dishonor

THREE ACES: excess

TWO ACES: enemies

THE ACES

The Aces of the minor arcana reveal new themes in life. They signify beginnings, action, and opportunities.

ACE OF CUPS

UPRIGHT MEANING
The suit of Cups is associated with the element of Water, the symbol of flowing emotions. It can signify a new passion, love and partnership, creativity, pregnancy and motherhood.

REVERSED MEANING
When reversed, the Ace shows emotions suppressed or out of control, so unhappiness or fears about a relationship may cause concern.

ACE OF PENTACLES

UPRIGHT MEANING
The suit of Pentacles takes the element of Earth, so the Ace brings money and opportunities, such as a new home or job.

REVERSED MEANING
The Ace reversed can reveal an obsession with money that masks a lack, or neglect, of other responsibilities, so priorities are skewed.

ACE OF WANDS

UPRIGHT MEANING

The suit of Wands represents negotiation and creativity. The card reveals the blossoming of new ventures, favoring travel, beginning a new career, or starting a family.

REVERSED MEANING

The reversed Ace can reveal delays, miscommunication, or a lack of commitment.

ACE OF SWORDS

UPRIGHT MEANING

The suit of Swords relates to the element of Air, which is associated with the realm of the intellect. When this card appears in a reading, it shows that your mental agility will bring you success. The Ace also predicts a time of challenge and possible conflict that forces you into action. The Ace brings success, new energy, and personal breakthroughs.

REVERSED MEANING

In the reversed position, the Ace of Swords reveals that you are being held back in some way, which leads to frustration and delay.

THE TWOS

Twos stand for balance, partnerships, and the flow of energy between opposite or compatible forces. The Two cards can show a pending decision or harmonious alignment, depending on their particular suit. With Wands, for example, the suit of negotiation and creativity, the Two reveals progress; with the martial Swords, the Two suggests procrastination or a truce, while the Two of Pentacles denotes choices.

TWO OF CUPS

UPRIGHT MEANING

The upright Two predicts natural harmony between two people. It reveals happy agreements and love, so a relationship may be sealed by an engagement or marriage. Two also sees friendships flourish as you instinctively know how to support and laugh with those around you.

REVERSED MEANING

The Two reversed indicates secrets and possibly betrayal. If you are considering a commitment to a partner, it is better to delay your decision until you can really talk with one another. This is a testing time for all relationships.

TWO OF PENTACLES

UPRIGHT MEANING

This Two represents balance and cashflow—as money comes in and goes out, you may need to prioritize certain payments. In broader terms, this is the card of choices, showing a decision about, for example, a location, study, or work.

REVERSED MEANING

The Two can reveal an unworkable liaison—a colleague or manager may not deliver what they claim. Viewed as an indication of a situation rather than an individual, a new venture may not take off due to lack of funding, which leads to worry and frustration. Take this card as a warning to examine the motives of those whom you choose to trust.

TWO OF WANDS

UPRIGHT MEANING

You are moving forward; those who have influence are listening to what you have to say. This card represents ideas and planning, and seeing opportunities that will lead to future success and stability. The Two also denotes trust and partnerships that bring reward.

REVERSED MEANING

The Two reversed can predict misplaced trust in an unreliable partner: a lover, work friend, or associate. This, as in all the reversed Twos, is the imbalance to watch out for. Expect others to meet you halfway.

TWO OF SWORDS

UPRIGHT MEANING

The Two of Swords can be taken literally, as someone you cross swords with in potential conflict. However, it is also a resting position before and after a battle of wits, and, in this sense, the Two reveals a truce or a stalemate; more generally, the card shows procrastination.

REVERSED MEANING

The Two reversed reveals a deception, often concerning a partnership. The stalemate of the upright card goes deeper here, as an opponent uses his or her time to manipulate the truth. When this card appears in a reading, it is best not to accept someone else's findings.

THE THREES

One, two, three: go. Three is the point at which everything begins, from blowing out candles on a cake to running a race. Three is the number of creation and life, the dynamic synthesis of primal one and balanced two.

As with the other number cards, the suit elements define how the Threes are expressed. In the fiery suit of Wands, the Three sees the development of an idea into reality; the feudal Three of Swords, with its element of Air for decisions and conflict, can foretell heartbreak.

THREE OF CUPS

UPRIGHT MEANING
This is a card of great happiness and a renewed belief in love. Your relationships and those of the people around you develop, so the atmosphere is joyful. Given the harmony of this card, it also brings healing and recovery to those who have felt at a low ebb. It reveals new energy and life, and can also foretell a new baby, project, or a celebration.

REVERSED MEANING
This reversed Three brings distance and discord. Disappointment or emotional betrayal creates a barrier in partnerships. The happiness in the upright card is dissipated, so there may be disappointment and disbelief.

THREE OF PENTACLES

UPRIGHT MEANING

You can now do what you do best. This is a time of tangible, early success, when hard work and application bring reward in terms of finances, but also creative satisfaction. You can feel pleased with your achievement because it is the result of your personal effort and vision.

REVERSED MEANING

There is an element of a project—or life in general—that you cannot face just now: the work itself. You want to have the fruits of your labor without the labor, or perhaps an ideal is blinding you to the reality. Consider that poor planning or rushing to complete the least interesting aspects of a job may be at the root of this.

THREE OF WANDS

UPRIGHT MEANING

This is a time of personal gain and reward when you let others see what motivates you through your work. The Three presents an inspired opportunity for self-expression through art, music, dance, travel, and crafts.

REVERSED MEANING

The Three reversed tells of a breakdown in communication. This card shows an inability to express your ideas, along with frustrating delays to projects and plans. In this situation, it may be best to slow your pace—declutter your thinking and simplify your plans until this influence shifts.

THREE OF SWORDS

UPRIGHT MEANING

The Three of Swords reveals tears, loss, and heartbreak. The Three of Swords can show three people in a relationship, so the card also suggests affairs and betrayal. Alternatively, another dream you held close to your heart is no longer feasible. The clarity of the card, however, clears the way for better times ahead.

REVERSED MEANING

In the reversed position, heartbreak is accompanied by quarreling and general disorder. Although this sounds more negative, expressing the upheaval can at least release and relieve the tension.

THE FOURS

Fours are even and stable. Four is the number of sides of a square, an ancient symbol for Earth in India and China. Four relates to structure: the four-armed cross, the four principal compass points, the four elements, and to the organization of the Tarot itself. There are four suits in the deck and four Court cards per suit, leaving forty numbered or "pip" cards.

In a reading, the Fours reveal practical situations rather than esoteric matters. They indicate stability or rigidity, depending again on the qualities of the particular suit.

FOUR OF CUPS

UPRIGHT MEANING

The Four of Cups shows a stuck situation or relationship. This may be temporary, but for the partnership to grow you need to revaluate what brought you together and go forward as one or both of you may be feeling restless or mildly bored. It's time to find the energy and inspiration you need.

REVERSED MEANING

In the reversed position, the Four indicates instability and deadlock, which drains your energy. You may submerge yourself in work or other time-hungry activities to avoid confronting a suffocating situation or relationship.

FOUR OF PENTACLES

UPRIGHT MEANING
Financial security is the message of the upright Four.
You may have suffered hardship and have had to work
too hard and for too long, and now your input pays off,
bringing satisfaction and reward. This card comes with a
caution, however, against materialism.

REVERSED MEANING
The Four reversed shows struggle. This may be because
you cannot believe that money may come easily to you
and that you are deserving of it. There may be financial
instability, and issues with management at work or home.

FOUR OF WANDS

UPRIGHT MEANING
This card is for a great social life, holidays, and happiness. As the Wands
bud with ideas, you may be inspired to move to a new home, extend your
existing dwelling, or simply spend time in a place you
love. Workwise, others show their appreciation of
your originality.

REVERSED MEANING
The Four reversed reveals the restrictive meaning of the
Fours: narrow attitudes block your route to success and
may make you feel invisible. As others actively progress
and are praised, you feel you don't fit in. Decide what or
whom needs to change.

FOUR OF SWORDS

UPRIGHT MEANING

The Four in this difficult suit means neutrality; for once, nothing is happening: no conflict or strife, but equally, no passion. It denotes rest and recuperation—this may be physical illness from which you can now recover, or time out from a relationship or job.

REVERSED MEANING

Whereas the upright Four is a welcome rest, the reversed Four imposes time away. This creates a sense of isolation and possibly resentment that blurs the benefits you may get from being away from home or work.

THE FIVES

Five is the number of mankind. The five-pointed star is the template for the form of an outstretched human being, with the head, hands, and feet marking each segment. The problems we encounter are manmade—we suffer for them, but can easily extricate ourselves.

Unusually, Fives have a similar meaning in all the minor arcana suits. A Five reveals a test: in the suit of Cups this is a test of emotional strength; in Wands, of capability; in Pentacles, of resources; and in Swords, a test of will.

FIVE OF CUPS

UPRIGHT MEANING
The Five of Cups is the natural outcome of the restless Four. Because small problems in a relationship have been neglected in the past, deeper doubt has taken root. This card can often indicate a relationship breaking up, or at least a time of separation when you both take time out to revaluate your partnership. Additional meanings include a loss, such as bereavement.

REVERSED MEANING
The Five of Cups is one of the few minor arcana cards that has a more positive meaning when reversed. This card reveals that you have reached the lowest point in a particular cycle; you have suffered, but are now further on in the healing process.

FIVE OF PENTACLES

UPRIGHT MEANING

The obvious meaning of this Five is being poor and feeling lost. It denotes financial difficulties, debt, and its associated stress, but bear in mind that the Five often mirrors a fear of losing money, friendship, or love, rather than actual scarcity. Know that this situation will pass.

REVERSED MEANING

A poor decision leaves you feeling impoverished. This applies both to finances and to relationships, so equally you may be on the receiving end of a partner's selfishness, which ultimately endangers your partnership. Reconsider your priorities, as your values are under scrutiny.

FIVE OF WANDS

UPRIGHT MEANING
The Five of Wands shows challenges to your position, and you may feel you are not being listened to. The message here is to remain steadfast rather than instill calm and appease others. The card can also signify exams and sports contests.

REVERSED MEANING
This Five carries the message of deception. You are hemmed in by another's dishonesty and there is little you can do to change the course of events, other than be clear that you are not to blame.

FIVE OF SWORDS

UPRIGHT MEANING
What exactly are you fighting for? This challenge can only deplete you, and you cannot win. It may be difficult to abandon the cause, but the Five of Swords indicates that it is time to walk away. The card traditionally shows oppression, humiliation, and, potentially, bullying. Now the outcome is clear, you can make plans elsewhere.

REVERSED MEANING
When the Five is in the reversed position, the conflict is either intensified, or not genuine—purely a show of strength or ego to cover up frailty or incompetence. See the situation for what it is, and move on.

THE SIXES

After the tumultuous Fives, the Sixes denote harmony and passivity. Sixes and fours can be difficult for new readers to differentiate. Imagine that Four signifies order and structure, whereas Six is its natural progression: contentment and balance.

As with all minor arcana cards, the element of each suit modifies the meaning. In the emotional suit of Cups, Six reveals the past meeting the present; in the fiery Six of Wands, we see achievement and recognition.

SIX OF CUPS

UPRIGHT MEANING

When the Six of Cups appears in your reading, memories resurface and you reconnect with people from your past. Mentally, this may be a time when you flit in and out of two worlds: your nostalgic past and happy present. In general, this is a time to appreciate what experience has taught you, and enjoy a new lease of life.

REVERSED MEANING

When the Six of Cups is reversed, a touch of nostalgia becomes sentimentality, along with a refusal to move on from the past. This may be expressed as clinginess toward others, or absorption in their needs to the exclusion of yours.

SIX OF PENTACLES

UPRIGHT MEANING

The upright Six of Pentacles shows that there is a beneficent understanding between you and those people who are close to you. During this happy phase you attract genuine help from above—for example, you may receive investment funding for a business from a mentor, a small cash sum, or an unexpected gift from a good friend.

REVERSED MEANING

As the upright Six reveals support and abundance, so the reversed card indicates meanness of spirit and financial withdrawal. It is advisable not to accept what little is on offer; hold out for the full amount, or write off the debt rather than buy into a deal or situation that compromises your values.

SIX OF WANDS

UPRIGHT MEANING

The upright Six of Wands brings success, deserved rewards, and recognition. This may be the favorable resolution of a legal matter, passing exams, or winning a promotion or new contract. However, this card comes with a small caution: examine carefully any offers in hand to ensure that all promises made will be fulfilled.

REVERSED MEANING

The Six of Wands reversed foretells delays to plans and a fear about their outcome. However, this does not mean you suffer from outright failure—simply a truly frustrating wait, during which you try to discover the right outlet for your dreams.

SIX OF SWORDS

UPRIGHT MEANING

The upright Six indicates peace of mind after trouble. You move away from stress, and may travel, for work or pleasure. This gives you a chance to breathe again and refuel your energy; it may even lead to a valuable discovery of some kind. Relax, and return with energy and enthusiasm.

REVERSED MEANING

The Six of Swords reversed can reveal a missed opportunity. As a result, the world shrinks rather than expands, and you feel in limbo. This card can also warn that you cannot rest just now; a retreat—the gift of this card in the upright position—may not be available just now.

THE SEVENS

Sacred to the god Apollo, the inspiration for the famous Delphic oracle, Seven has a reputation as a mystical number. It's also seen as the number of potential because it is made from three (the number for heaven) and four (for Earth), indicating the possibility of greatness through integration. In a reading, consider that all the Sevens share this theme of potential and the need for integrity and perception.

SEVEN OF CUPS

UPRIGHT MEANING
The Seven of Cups reveals that you may question a recent offer. You are following a dream, but make sure that this opportunity will deliver. Confusion and indecision abound with this card, so you have only your instinct to rely upon. This is a time of great creativity; just be sure that whatever you are dealing with is right for you.

REVERSED MEANING
The reversed Seven indicates the danger of idealizing a person or situation in order to avoid an unpalatable truth. You may be so keen to succeed, or your desires so overwhelming, that you delude yourself. The message is not to take anything for granted.

SEVEN OF PENTACLES

UPRIGHT MEANING
The Seven of Pentacles tells you that you must keep on going, because there is more on offer. Work on a long-term project looks promising, but it is not time to rest yet—plans will come to fruition, but only with steady application and willpower.

REVERSED MEANING
Like the upright Seven of Pentacles, the reversed card also reveals the need to act. However, this is because progress is non-existent: time has been wasted, and money problems may be the result of doing too little too late.

SEVEN OF WANDS

UPRIGHT MEANING
Just as the Seven of Pentacles urges action, so the Seven of Wands shows the need to keep talking, and stay true to your values, in spite of all the difficult debate or arguments around you.

REVERSED MEANING
In the reversed position, the Seven shows serious concerns about the work you are doing. A project or current contract may feel unworkable and without purpose, which in turn causes you to doubt your position.

SEVEN OF SWORDS

UPRIGHT MEANING

As the Sevens indicate the need for perception, the martial Seven of Swords calls for an expert plan to disarm an adversary. You may be feeling cornered, but your intellect may prove to be your best ally. The watchwords are protection and strategy, to safeguard what you value. Double-check home security and keep valuables close.

REVERSED MEANING

The Seven of Swords reversed can reveal that you give up on a fight too soon. Be adamant about what you want, and be prepared to make a forceful stand for it rather than give in to others' manipulation.

THE EIGHTS

The Eights in the minor arcana signify change. This may appear inconsistent with the other even numbers—two, four, and six—which indicate stability, as the natural tension of opposites is balanced. However, as the numbered minor arcana suits run from the Aces to the completion of the Tens, the Eights hold the history of our experience. With this accumulation, decisions beckon. Although change can bring anxiety, its purpose is renewal. Baptismal fonts have eight sides as a symbol of regeneration.

In the Eights, there is also the need for assessment and judgment based on self-acceptance. The Eight of Cups, for example, denotes a change of heart.

EIGHT OF CUPS

UPRIGHT MEANING
The Eight of Cups indicates change. This may relate to a change of heart in a relationship or another situation that can progress no further. There may be no fault with the other party, but you turn away to seek what you need elsewhere. This is a decision you take to protect yourself in the long term.

REVERSED MEANING
As you might expect, the reversed Eight of Cups shows an error of judgment. You may walk away from an established relationship or other opportunity because you cannot appreciate its worth; or you find yourself the victim of someone else's poor judgment.

EIGHT OF PENTACLES

UPRIGHT MEANING
The Eight reveals money and reward for talent
and skill. A further meaning is qualifications and
success in examinations. Overall, this Eight stands
for professionalism and perfectionism, and you hold
yourself to high standards.

REVERSED MEANING
Restriction: being in the wrong place or position, which
makes you doubt your ambition and direction. The Eight
reversed can also show that you are motivated solely by
money, possibly because a soul-destroying project or work has little else to offer.

EIGHT OF WANDS

UPRIGHT MEANING
The Eight of Wands brings news. This is a fast and frantic time when
communication is key and opportunities and offers come in. You may travel,
partake in a creative collaboration, be inspired by talking to stimulating
individuals, or contribute to a community project. If you
are waiting for answers, this card tells you "yes."

REVERSED MEANING
In the reversed position, the Eight of Wands shows a
degree of confusion because you cannot seem to connect
with those you want to deal with, or be clear about what
they want. When you try to communicate, you miss the
mark: texts, messages, and emails disappear.

EIGHT OF SWORDS

UPRIGHT MEANING

The Eight is the card of restriction. It can signify a setback and, more generally, a way of thinking. In love relationships, the card can show that one partner is unavailable, physically and/or emotionally, so the relationship is restricted, hidden, or one-sided.

REVERSED MEANING

The Eight of Swords reversed reveals frustration. You may feel furious with yourself and lash out at others because you need an outlet for your inability to accept a difficult situation. The way out is to drop your defences; telling the truth frees you to see a way out.

THE NINES

Nines are known as the "ultimates" of their suits, where the intrinsic value of each suit finds maximum expression. Nine represents the triple triad of mind, body, and spirit; it also expresses order and spiritual integration.

With the Nines, it is helpful to recall the suit element meanings and develop them to their utmost. As Cups represent water and the emotions, the Nine crowns you with wishes fulfilled, while Earth-bound Pentacles reveal a material gain. As ever, the troublesome Swords represent conflict—in Nine, an accumulation of thoughts, resulting in unrest.

NINE OF CUPS

UPRIGHT MEANING
The Nine of Cups is often referred to as the "wish card" in a reading. It means that a dream may come true; everything you hope for can become reality. This abundant card shows a surfeit of affection and fun, and a perfect balance in all your relationships. This is a time for socializing, new friendships, and romantic partnerships.

REVERSED MEANING
In the reversed position, the Nine shows imbalance in the realm of the affections. You may distance yourself from those in your social circle, or feel sidelined due to another person's self-absorption. Overall, there's a sense of emotional disconnection.

NINE OF PENTACLES

UPRIGHT MEANING
The Nine of Pentacles shows a time for reward and luxuries. You have achieved material stability through hard work and financial acumen, and now you have time for leisure. Your sense of contentment is attractive to others, so be prepared for a meeting of minds.

REVERSED MEANING
Your domestic sanctuary may be under siege when the Nine of Pentacles reverses. Irresponsibility with money, or an unwillingness to deal with debts or confront disputes, leaves you vulnerable to feelings of insecurity.

NINE OF WANDS

UPRIGHT MEANING
You are in a strong position. However, the card asks you to be efficient, to use your energy and resources wisely in order to keep going. In friendships and relationships, you may need to be discerning about whom you let in to your circle. A further meaning is trust issues due to past hurt.

REVERSED MEANING
The Nine reversed suggests relentless demands on your time. You may need to focus on yourself, rather than appease others.

NINE OF SWORDS

UPRIGHT MEANING

Whereas many of the Swords cards depict suffering in external situations, the Nine is concerned with internal processes. It can mean stress and worry, which may take the form of anxiety about the future, worry about the self or others, nightmares, insomnia, or random, anxious thoughts. A further meaning is physical pain or discomfort that disturbs sleep.

REVERSED MEANING

Unfortunately, the reversed Nine of Swords intensifies the experience of anxiety associated with the upright card. In this instance there may be feelings of despair and entrapment. However, you can get through this testing time. Ask for help and you can find a way to restore your faith.

THE TENS

Tens stand for completeness and perfection. Ten is also a mystic number with myriad examples of its importance—the Ten Commandments of the Old Testament; the astrological decan, or ten degrees of a zodiac sign, as a predictor of personality types. With number Ten a cycle is complete and begins again, so Ten encompasses both endings and beginnings.

The Ten of Wands reveals the weight of the world on your shoulders; in Cups, the love of family; in the suit of Swords, the focus moves from the individual in conflict to endings; and in Pentacles, the Ten represents the most that money and security can bring.

TEN OF CUPS

UPRIGHT MEANING
The Ten of Cups signifies love and complete contentment in relationships. The Ten brings a sense of perfect togetherness and achievement, and an appreciation of your place at home and in the wider world. An additional meaning is finding your ideal home.

REVERSED MEANING
The Ten reversed expresses disruption to your social circle. Consider that this card can arise if you are afraid of losing someone, and when there is a feeling of unrest due to something being taken from a family or group.

TEN OF PENTACLES

UPRIGHT MEANING
The Ten of Pentacles in the upright position reveals inheritance, generosity, and possibly a love match that brings a wealth of love and happiness. The flavor of this card is also maturity, in terms of maturing investment policies, and also emotional wisdom. This is a time to enjoy abundance.

REVERSED MEANING
Inevitably, the Ten reversed shows adversity concerning family money and property, and can reveal a love mismatch. There is a rigidity implied here too, where the expectations of older generations clash with those of younger members.

TEN OF WANDS

UPRIGHT MEANING

If the Ten of Wands is the first card to appear in a reading, you may want to reshuffle the deck and lay the cards again; the Ten is often a signal that you are overburdened and need to take more time in order to be receptive to the reading. The meaning of the Ten is that you are carrying the weight of the world, with all its attendant pressures.

REVERSED MEANING

The Ten of Wands reversed is a message that you need to lighten up, for the burdens that you carry are more imagined than actual. You may believe that others' demands on you are the sole cause of your predicament, but it may be easier to blame them than destroy the illusion of your own importance. When you stop diverting your energies to the needs of others, you will be able to care for yourself more effectively.

TEN OF SWORDS

UPRIGHT MEANING

The Ten of Swords means sudden endings and change. It brings truth, and a release from uncertainty; you can see your situation exactly as it is. In work, this may mark the end of a relationship, job, or contract. The message is that it is best to accept this necessary conclusion.

REVERSED MEANING

In the reversed position, the meaning of the upright card stands. However, because more strife is unfortunately to come, you may feel besieged by worry. The world will turn, and you with it.

THE PAGES

The Pages of the minor arcana are usually described as young people or children. Pages can also represent young situations, or new influences in your life. The type of influence is determined according to the element of each suit—emotional, idealistic, financial, or intellectual.

PAGE OF CUPS

UPRIGHT MEANING
The Page of Cups is a sociable, intuitive spirit who just loves good company and the good life. As a messenger, the Page has positive news about relationships and children. His presence can be reassuring, particularly if he arrives after a spell of emotional insecurity.

REVERSED MEANING
The reversed Page is a young person who is unable to express his feelings. As a message, the card can reveal miscommunication, frustration, and emotional blocks.

PAGE OF PENTACLES

UPRIGHT MEANING
The reliable and responsible Page brings good news about money. As a message, the card asks you to tend to your finances. A further meaning is beginning an educational course.

REVERSED MEANING
The Page reversed signifies mistrust and irresponsibility with money. The message is that someone may be taking more than their share.

PAGE OF WANDS

UPRIGHT MEANING
The Wands bring conversations and conditions for success, so this Page is an inventive youth who is a natural communicator. As a message, the card says an offer is coming, and you will soon have news. The advice is to take up this opportunity, but do check the details first.

REVERSED MEANING
The Page reversed can show a young person who is not communicative, and who may have difficulties with self-expression. As a message, promises may not be kept.

PAGE OF SWORDS

UPRIGHT MEANING

Bright beyond their years, the Page of Swords has wit and perception. They bring good intelligence, along with helpful people who take swift action to help your cause. As a message, the card's meaning is to stay sharp; a further interpretation is signing documents.

REVERSED MEANING

The reversed Page is secret poison, manipulating people through misinformation and lies. As a message, the card signifies disruption, unfairness, or poor judgment.

THE KNIGHTS

The Knights are the seekers of the minor arcana, symbolizing action. The quality of this action depends upon the suit element. The Knight of Cups, with his element of Water, may prefer words and romantic ideals—a potential conflict with the traditional role of Knight. The fiery, impulsive Knight of Wands is characterized by urgency and speed, but his influence may be fleeting as his interest burns bright, then burns out. The more placid Knight of Pentacles prefers to plod rather than race, while the Knight of Wands brings drama and battle.

KNIGHT OF CUPS

UPRIGHT MEANING

This Knight is a dreamy, affectionate individual who brings new friends for you. As a potential lover, however, his lack of action may leave you confused. As a situation, the card can simply mean an offer or proposal.

REVERSED MEANING

The negative traits of the upright Knight of Cups are magnified in the reversed position: this Knight cannot keep a promise. As a broader situation, the card denotes disappointment.

KNIGHT OF PENTACLES

UPRIGHT MEANING

The Knight of Pentacles comes with a guarantee: travel with him and you get where you need to go. Pragmatic and loyal, he makes slow and steady progress. As a situation, the card reveals that your consistent effort will pay off, particularly in regard to education and finances.

REVERSED MEANING

The Knight reversed is at best a ditherer and at worst a thief. It is therefore best to play detective when dealing with any new financial advisors or institutions; check the small print of all policies and other contracts.

KNIGHT OF WANDS

UPRIGHT MEANING

The Knight of Wands is a passionate, liberal character who gets things moving. As a situation, this Knight symbolizes a creative time during which decisions are made, and events speed up. A further meaning is moving house.

REVERSED MEANING

The Knight of Wands in the reversed position appears to make a contribution to an important project, but he is doing little. As a situation, the card advises caution.

KNIGHT OF SWORDS

UPRIGHT MEANING

The Knight has drive and charisma, but brings battles that must be fought. This card can be interpreted as stressful situations—arguments, opposition, and outbursts. On a more positive note, this Knight, as a fast mover in a suit famed for action, represents a great surge of energy.

REVERSED MEANING

The Knight of Swords warns that someone whom you rely upon cannot be trusted. As a situation, the card often suggests rivalry and feeling undermined.

THE QUEENS

Traditionally, the Queens represent the influences of women; in a reading, the Queen can represent a partner, or she may symbolize aspects of the self. The four Queens of the minor arcana can also be seen as four aspects of major arcana card III, the Empress: emotional and nurturing (Cups); creative and communicative (Wands); abundant and practical (Pentacles); and intelligent and protective (Swords).

QUEEN OF CUPS

UPRIGHT MEANING

The upright Queen of Cups is the Queen of Hearts: she represents love and natural beauty, and can symbolize the ideal partner. Sociable, sensitive, and artistic, emotions rule her world. Intuition and perception are also highlighted when she appears, so this is a time to take note of your dreams.

REVERSED MEANING

The Queen of Cups reversed is a competitive socialite who often thrives on other people's attention, yet she gives little in return. As a situation, she symbolizes deception and jealousy.

QUEEN OF PENTACLES

UPRIGHT MEANING

This Queen may appear in your life as a wise, supportive mentor. In a reading, she represents generosity, and can also show feeling closely connected with animals and the natural world.

REVERSED MEANING

When reversed, this Queen uses money as a weapon with which to control others. As a situation, the card represents financial insecurity.

QUEEN OF WANDS

UPRIGHT MEANING

This Queen has a magic wand with which to do her bidding. Sociable, forward-looking, and nurturing, she represents leadership, communication, and creativity, and asks you to speak your truth.

REVERSED MEANING

The Queen of Wands reversed takes on more than she can handle. She is overprotective, and wants involvement in order to feel included. As a situation, the card can show offers or help that do not materialize.

QUEEN OF SWORDS

UPRIGHT MEANING

This Queen is defined by her mental alacrity. Her company is stimulating and she uses her intelligence to entertain, enthrall, and challenge those around her. Forthright and graceful, she relies on logic and instinct to run her life. As an influence, she represents self-sufficiency.

REVERSED MEANING

The Queen reversed turns her sword on others, and may look for excuses to do so. These are the actions of a bitter individual who may pose as a moralist. As a situation, this reversed card can show extreme defensiveness due to stress.

THE KINGS

Traditionally, the Kings represent the influences of a mature man; in a reading, the King can represent a partner; or he may symbolize aspects of the self. The Kings of the minor arcana can also be seen as four aspects of card IV, the Emperor, who represents order and rulership. When applying this to the suits, we get the following correspondences: mastery of emotions (Cups); creativity and impulse (Wands); loyalty and protection (Pentacles); intellect and action (Swords).

KING OF CUPS

UPRIGHT MEANING
The King of Cups has sensitivity. As a master of emotions, however, he may suppress his feelings, which makes him appear distant. As a situation, the card signifies managing emotions, and problems solved.

REVERSED MEANING
The King of Cups reversed shows disruptive behaviors, such as a refusal to communicate. As a situation, the card reveals emotional fragility.

KING OF PENTACLES

UPRIGHT MEANING

The King of Pentacles in the upright position shows pride in achievement. Often a professional or business owner, he works hard to protect and support those close to him. As a situation, he heralds resolutions and reward.

REVERSED MEANING

The King of Pentacles reversed can be a dangerous opponent. It is important that he wins at all cost, and therefore is untrustworthy when dealing with any cause other than his own. A further meaning of the card is workaholism.

KING OF WANDS

UPRIGHT MEANING

The King of Wands has entrepreneurial spirit, a traveler who loves exploration and freedom. He is protective, but he understands others' needs to express themselves as individuals. As a situation, the card shows friendship, communication, and charisma.

REVERSED MEANING

The King reversed has a narrow mindset and may occur as an overbearing parent or boss. As a situation, he can signify resentment and egotism.

KING OF SWORDS

UPRIGHT MEANING

The King of Swords is a master of the mind; he relies on his wits and his ambition is clear. As a situation, he denotes actions such as legal rulings, strategies, and planning. In relationships, the card can reveal a lack of empathy.

REVERSED MEANING

The King of Swords reversed represents dangerous opposition. When he appears in a reading, you may be dealing with someone who will try to outwit you in any way he can, playing a cruel game of cat and mouse. It may be best to retreat than continue to oppose him.

INDEX

TAROT RESOURCES

BIBLIOGRAPHY

Ben-Dov, Yoav, *Tarot: The Open Reading* (CreateSpace, 2013)
Dean, Liz, *The Magic of Tarot* (CICO Books, 2019)
Dee, Jonathan, *Tarot: An Illustrated Guide* (D & S Books, 2000)
Douglas, Alfred, *The Tarot* (Penguin, 1988)
Fenton, Sasha, *Fortune Telling by Tarot Cards* (Zambezi Publishing, 2002)
Kaplan, Stuart R., *The Encyclopedia of Tarot (Vol. I)* (U.S. Games Systems, Inc., 2001)
Ozaniec, Naomi, *Initiation into the Tarot* (Watkins Publishing, 2002)
Pollack, Rachel, *The Complete Illustrated Guide to Tarot* (Element Books, 1999)
Sharman-Burke, Juliet, *The Complete Book of Tarot* (Pan Books, 1985)
Simon, Sylvie, *The Tarot: Art, Mysticism, and Divination* (Alpine Fine Arts Collection, 1986)
Tilley, Roger, *A History of Playing Cards* (Studio Vista, 1973)
Waite, Arthur Edward, *The Pictorial Key to the Tarot* (Samuel Weiser, Inc., 2000)

AUTHOR WEBSITE

www.lizdean.info

ACKNOWLEDGMENT

With thanks to all at CICO Books.

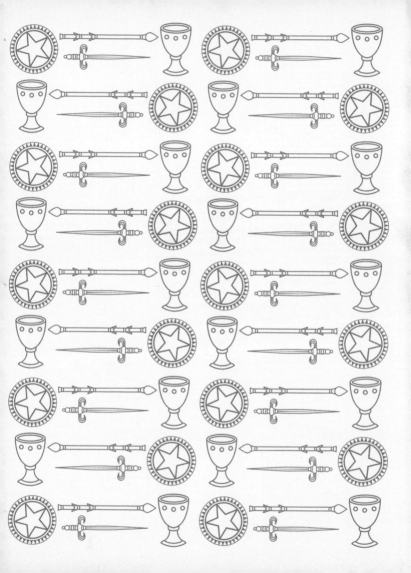